PRESS OPINIONS

"A must. . . . There is no other way to appreciate missing this book."
> —Edward Cleverley
> in *The Manhattan Daily Post*

"Stunningly illiterate—unequaled for sheer unintelligibility."
> —Pergola Pox
> in *New Misdirections*

"A consternation devoutly to be wished."
> —Hamlet Solus
> in *The Tutor Times*

"If this be reason make the most of it!"
> —Henry Patrick
> in *The Virginia Monthly Inquirer*

From Beowulf to Virginia Woolf

A LITERARY MAP
OF THE BRITISH ISLES

Miles

0   50   100   150   200   250

Bodley Head

Boswell Field

SILVER

SEA

Wed Loch
Ward Loch
Yale Loch
Rape Loch
Loch Slee
Hall

The Hence of Forth

Chapman Hall
McGraw Hill
Longman's Green

Heath Cliff   Fingal's Cave

Macmillan-
the-Floss

Lake
Eerie

THE
PURITAN
INTERLEWD

Burnt Gidding

Third Forth

EYRE

Spottiswoode

Rin-tin-tin's
Abbey

SUSSEX

Some Bridge

Bard-on-Avon

NOSSEX

Um Bridge

THE SLOT

Upper Plate
over Stourbridge

MIDDLESEX

Pepys' Dairy

Lady Windermere's
Farm

Upsom Downs

Jonathan Cape

Drake's Bowling
Alley

FROM BEOWULF
TO VIRGINIA WOOLF

An Astounding and Wholly Unauthorized
History of English Literature

by

Robert Manson Myers, Ph.D. (Oxen)

NEW EDITION

THOROUGHLY DEVISED

DIFFUSELY ILLUSTRATED

University of Illinois Press
Urbana and Chicago

NOTE

Acknowledgment is made to The Viking Press, Inc., for their permission
to adapt several of the boners in their series of *Boners* books for inclusion
in this volume.

Acknowledgment is also made to the Trustees of the National Gallery,
London, for their permission to reproduce the following paintings:
"Jealousy," by Cranach (p. 5); "Marcus Curtius (?)," by Bacchiacca
(p. 6); "Pan and Syrinx," by Balen (p. 9); "The Saints and Blessed of the
Dominican Order" (detail), by Angelico (p. 12); "A Concert," by Costa
(p. 15); "Portrait of Jan Arnolfini and Jeanne de Chenany His Wife"
(detail), by Van Eyck (p. 19); "Judith and Holofernes," by Santvoort
(p. 22); "Roger Delivering Angelica," by Ingres (p. 28); "Three Portraits
of Cardinal Richelieu," by Champaigne (p. 34); "Susannah and the El-
ders," by Carracci (p. 37); "Portrait of Lucas Fayd'herbe (?)," by Fran-
choijs (p. 41); "A Woman Bathing," by Rembrandt (p. 44); "Cattle and
Figures: The Large Dort" (detail), by Cuyp (p. 47); "Marriage à la Mode:
Shortly after the Marriage" (detail), by Hogarth (p. 51); "The Judgment
of Paris" (detail), by Rubens (p. 54); "The Shrimp Girl," by Hogarth
(p. 57); "Venus Surprised by Satyrs," by Nicolas Poussin (p. 62); "Oedipus
and the Sphinx," by Ingres (p. 72); "An Angel," by the School of Bot-
ticelli (p. 75); "Venus, Cupid, Folly, and Time," by Bronzino (p. 81);
"Head of a Girl," by Greuze (p. 82); "Bacchanalian Festival," by Nicolas
Poussin (p. 86).

Acknowledgment is also made to the Trustees of the Tate Gallery, London, for their permission to reproduce the following paintings: "Sea Off
Brighton" (detail), by Constable (p. 27); "Monna Vanna," by Rossetti
(p. 78); "Woman with a Bag," by Schmidt-Rottluff (p. 89).

"The Portrait of a Lady," by Francis van der Mijn (p. 65), is reproduced
from the collection of Robert Manson Myers.

This book is printed on acid-free paper.

Library of Congress Cataloging in Publication Data

Myers, Robert Manson, 1921–
From Beowulf to Virginia Woolf.

1. English literature—History and criticism—
Anecdotes, Facetiae, satire, etc.   I. Title.
PR86.M9   1984   827'.009   84-5974
ISBN 0-252-01126-0

To My Mother and Father
Who Made All This Possible

FOREWORD

OVER TWO CENTURIES ago Alexander Pope observed that "fools rush in where Anglophiles fear to tread." It is therefore only at the insistence of an admiring public that I once again emerge from literary retirement. In an age of skyscrapers, television, and hydraulic bombs it is appalling that the average undergraduate is scarcely able to distinguish the passive tense from the simple futility of a common English verb. And in the light of current events it is probable that conditions throughout Europe are even more serious. Be that as it may (and it usually is), the need for a definitive survey of the wolf motif in English literature has long been felt by scholars and intelligentsia alike.

To meet this need I here present, from a strictly fresh point of view, the unspeakable literary contribution of the British Empire before and since the publication of *Lyrical Ballast* in 1798. Following a roughly chronological scheme, I analyze the One Hundred and One Best Poets against the hysterical background of their time. Readers acquainted with my former work will, I trust, find this new volume a striking departure from the usual survey of English literature. My scope is tremendous: in ten brief chapters I range from "The She-Wolf" and "Dyed in the Wolf" to "The Warp and the Wolf" and "The Big Bad Wolf."

The present study grew out of a doctoral disputation written at a fashionable eastern finishing school; it appears now only after expensive revision at the Harvard Theological Cemetery and the British Mausoleum. For the reader's convenience footnotes have been microfilmed and are available under separate cover upon bequest.

To the instructor it is suggested that the classroom be seated in algebraic order and kept constantly on the verge of mental exertion through the use of provocative questions. What, for instance, *does* the Golden Mean? What *was* the age of Pope? Of Elizabeth Barrett Browning? Who *is* Silvia? What was the position of women under the Greeks?

Grateful acknowledgment is hereby extended to Professor Carrie Coles, of Newcastle, who uncovered for me the bare facts of Lord Byron's secret love affair with Jane Austen; to the late Professor Dewberry Oldberry of the Newberry Library for extremely rare pamphlets detailing the teetotali-tarianism of John Drinkwater; and to Professor W. K. Kellogg for assistance with the Union List of Serials.

For various favors I am also indebted to Si-gnorina Angelina Torso, of Itchyng Palms, Florida; to Mademoiselle Bibi du Bibelot, of Shady Deal, Texas; to Louise Fallopian, Ph.D., of New Fangle, Connecticut; to Optimus Swivett, Esquire, of Scro-tum Hall, Yorkshire; and to the Honourable Peter Pounce.

A more personal word of gratitude I should like to express to my secretary, who has requested that I withhold her name from the index. My thanks are also due to my wife, without whose unfailing insis-tence an index would not have been impossible.

Portions of Chapters Six and Seven first appeared in *Harper's Bizarre* and are reprinted here by kind permission of the publisher.

It scarcely seems necessary for me to add that any similarity in this volume to any person living and dead is strictly confidential.

R. M. M.

All Fools' Day, 1984

CONTENTS

ILLUSTRATIONS

Illustrations (cont.)

From Beowulf to Virginia Woolf

KEY TO ABBREVIATIONS

BAA: Beowulf Association of America
EATS: Early American Text Society
IQ: Icelandic Quarterly
ODE: Oxford Dictionary of English
*PAMELA: Publications of the American Muddle English
    Language Association*
RFD: Royal French Documents

CHAPTER ONE

The Wolf at the Door

Who's afraid of the big Beowulf?
—Ye Olde Anguische Carol

AT THE DOOR of English literature stands Beowulf, the great Dane, who once upon a time inhabited the forest primevil with Ethelwulf, his wife, and is therefore known as "The Noble Savage." It would, of course, be disproportionate to dwell on Beowulf's particulars in a brief survey such as this, especially since those particulars are fully recorded in Beowulf's autobiographical beast epic, first published in 1066 as *The Doomsday Book*. This tame tome was printed, curiously enough, from a cotton manuscript, destroyed by fire in 1731 and later purchased from descendants of the Beowulf family by the American philanderer Andrew Carnegie. Unfortunately the original duodecimo is totally ineligible. After centuries of scholarship, however, it has finally emerged that Beowulf, together with his brother,

3

Cynewulf, sailed forth boldly into the filth and froth of the Firth of Forth in the spring of 596 A.D. Following his slaughter of Grendel (a task as odious as Oedipus' cleansing of the Aegean stables), the epic hero retraced his footsteps across the sea. His spritely narrative abounds with exploits of Half-Dane, High-Shellac, Wroth-Child, and other forebears of the Three Bears.[1]

Since England is located on the coast of Great Britain and therefore not far from the sea, she has always been subject to continental influences. Christianity was introduced by the Romans in 55 B.C.; and it was not long before England was overrun by Angels, Sextons, and Jukes, as well as by swarms of Picks, Scotts, and Dames, who settled north of the Humber River near the Ooze. The Picks, Scotts, and Dames were ignorant, uniformed people who, living in the Stone Age, took everything for granite; they went so far in their hedonism (a strangely violent form of heathenism) as to worship Weird, or Fate. The Angels and Sextons were superstitious people who still worshiped ghosts, goblins, virgins, and other supernatural monsters. But the Jukes were sensible people who followed the so-called Sa-

1. BAA: 596.

4

THE FOREST PRIMEVIL

Beowulf, the Great Dane, thrashes Grendel
while Ethelwulf, the Noble Savage, turns her back
By kind permission of Lord Piltdown

CAESAREAN PAUSE

Ethelred the Unread rides forth on his *horse de combat*
to Caesar's Pubic Wars
By kind permission of Lady Edyth Tooting-Bec

line Law, a primitive compilation of Germane Law, according to which: (1) no man could be king if descended from a woman; and (2) one must take everything with a grain of salt.

Despite such astringent laws the British throne continued to thrive, and the line of English kings accordingly includes such familiar names as Old King Cole, Good King Wenceslas, and the King of the Golden River, all of whom flourished (or failed to flourish) about 700 A.D. In order to stimulate the production of ballads and epics Old King Cole passed the Danelaw, the Poor Law, and the Ancren Rule; and in order to encourage the creation of sagas Good King Wenceslas, although unmarried at the time, translated *The Forsyte Saga* into Ye Olde Anguische.[2]

Later Caedmon, a Medium High German monk of St. Edmunds, produced *The Dream of the Rude*, an ill-punctuated diatribe in Ye Olde Norse:

> Everich ladie in þe lande
> Haþ twentye nailes upon ech hande
> Five ande twentye on hande and fete
> And þis is trewe withouten deceite.[3]

2. See Balzac's *Troll Stories*.
3. Though this be madness, yet there is method in't.

7

Hostile criticism of this foolish doggerel gave rise to a fierce slogan: "Bury St. Edmunds" (presumably alive). Caedmon had been a pupil of the Venerable Bede, the Wolfsbane, whose spiritual autobiography, *Two Years Before the Mass*, explained how, as author of the Catholic *Missile*, Bede entered a monastery[4] and in two years became, relatively speaking, the father of English literature. He was tickled to death.[5]

Frequently Ye Olde Anguische verse was translated into Gnomic and recited by barges who traveled about the country. Such verse was rugged, unkempt, and usually marked by Caesarean pause. Its two chief exponents were Ethelred the Unread,[6] son of Eveready the Red and Ethel the Unready, and St. Wulfstan Wulfilas, a Goth from Gotham who, beholding a moat in his brother's eye, translated the Bible into Gothic.

If the Venerable Bede was the father of English literature, then certainly Alfred the Great was its eldest son. In early youth, prompted by his wife, Queen Mab, Alfred founded *The Anglo-Saxon*

---

4. Tintern Abbey, on the Isle of Wright, where the Hebrew Ark of the Convent was kept.

5. The standard biography is George Eliot's *Adam Bede*.

6. *IQ:* 58.

THE GUILT SYSTEM

Zarathustra, King Arthur's columbine,
flees from the wiles of Sin the Bad Sailor
By kind permission of Lady Bottoms

Chronicle, the first English mouth organ, which continued on and off for more than two hundred years. Meanwhile his nephew, King Arthur, having been washed up as a baby, married the Lady of Shalott, produced the Arthurized Version of the Bible, and founded the Order of the Knights of the Wife of Bath, with its cryptic motto: *Pas de lieu aune que nous*. Tales of adventure, especially in Arabia, were nightly related to King Arthur at the Crystal Palace by Zarathustra, one of his columbines, who, though she lived at the time with David Harem,[7] thus spake, seducing the king with stories of Sin the Bad Sailor, Alibi and the Forty Thieves, Sohrab and Rustum, Ozymandias and Lalla Rookh, and the Four Horsemen of the Acropolis. At King Arthur's round-table discussions gathered the flower of English knighthood (the Idols of the King), and there one might have beheld such flowers as Launcelot, Excalibur, Ivanhoe, Childe Roland, and of course the page boy Bob.

7. A Confederate Yankee at King Arthur's court.

CHAPTER TWO

The Big Bad Wolf

Pox vobiscum.

—Muddle Latin Proverb

HEN ONE GAZES at the grotesque gargles of an ancient gothic cathedral and appreciates the exquisite ratio and proportion of its towering minuets and flying buttocks, one realizes that it was only with the introduction of continental culture following the Norman Conquest that the Muddle Ages in England actually commenced. Time before 1066 is now reckoned as "Time In Memoriam." In that year William the Conqueror and his merry men defeated Childe Harold at the Battle of Warren Hastings, ruthlessly raised London to the ground, and immediately passed an edict forbidding all births, marriages, and deaths in England for a period of one year.

Later William established the Futile System, with its intricate relationships between lord, vessel, serf, and villain, according to which serfs, villains, and ar-

CAMBRIDGE MASS

St. Vincent Millay (*front row, extreme right*)
and Charlie the Chaplain (*back row, extreme left*)
worship with sundry others of the clerical choler
Courtesy of the Early English Textile Society

tesians, low forms of medevil life, were attached to the soil, so that when it moved they moved with it. But William's greatest contribution was the Guilt System, an organization designed to encourage arts and graft. It was England's foremost guild, the Early English Textile Society, that drew up the Mosaic Code ("A lie for a lie and a tooth for a tooth"), according to which medevil mosaic workers were permitted to send their children to the Merchant Sailors Mysteries.

William was, according to his usual custom, killed in battle,[1] after which he was forced to sign the Magna Carta, a famous document providing that: (1) no man should be imprisoned for debt so long as he had the money to pay; and (2) no free man should be hanged twice for the same offense.

In 878 Alfred the Great had passed the so-called "Grim" Law, according to which Ye Olde Anguische was to be superseded in 1066 by Muddle English. Thus overnight English accidents and grammar, though still somewhat illiterate, passed from infancy to adultery, with three genders (masculine, feline, and neutral) and eight parts of speech (nouns, pronouns, adjectives, propositions, verbs, adverbs, prov-

1. At Ganymede.

erbs, and irregular verbs).[2] From the Latin Muddle English derived five cases (nominal, genital, dated, accusative, and ablaut), and from Sanscript and Arabesque, the principal Semantic languages, it inherited the propositional phase and the tangling polysyllable.[3] And as a result of the Great Germanic Sound-Split, Ancient Illyrian *x* became Indo-Iranian *y*—except, of course, when preceded by a penultimate ablative obsolete.[4]

Against this frightful background Muddle English literature sprang up and even flourished. The Muddle Ages were fond of romance, and English writers, following the example of the Old High German *minnowsingers*, enrolled at the London School of Courtly Love (headed by Lord Geoffrey the Mammoth) and produced courtly tales now known as *chansons de beau geste*.[5] In these courtly tales women were no longer regarded as mere wives, mothers, and

2. Injections and interjunctions were obsolete by 878.
3. See Anna Coluthon, "The *Cum* Casual Clause in Muddle English," *PAMELA*, 19 (1919), 19. See also W. Cabell Greek's remarks on Krapp's *English Synonyms*.
4. For further illumination see F. P. McGoon, "Misinterpretations of Transcontinental Voiced Spirants During the Second Phase of Old Church Slavonic Periphrasis," *PAMELA*, 38 (1938), 38.
5. French love songs written by Roland.

GLORIA IN EXCELSIOR

Three Old High German *minnowsingers*
render *chansons de beau geste*
at the London School of Courtly Love
Courtesy of Countess Sobriquet

secondary creatures; the typical medevil *chanson* presents a succession of nightly adventures (such stuff as dreams are made on), loosely related in French octoslapstick couplets.

A popular figure in medevil romance was Joan of Arc, one of the Seven Wise (or Vested) Virgins, who became inspired after hearing angel voices singing *do re mi*. Richard the Iron-Hearted urged Joan to become his mistress, and when the brave girl, having once served as a maid in New Orleans, reclined to do so, she was cannonized (that is, beautified) by George Bernard Shaw; and her virtuous triumph is now celebrated as the Revolution of St. Joan the Divine.

Of the four great Middle Aged poets (Chaucer, Gore, Pearl the Poet, and the Peerless Plowman), Chaucer, a member of the English diplomatic corpse in France, was the first who dared forsake the classic Latin of his father to write in his mother's tongue. In early youth Chaucer edited *The Book of the Duchess* (the diary of the Duchess of Malfi) and wrote *The Hous of Il Fame,* a satire on love, women, and sex in general. Later he commenced *The Canterbury Tales*, a parchment of fools based upon Boccaccio's *Consolation of Boethius,* a collection of fourteenth-century pornographs. In 1066 an archbishop named St. Thomas Aquinas, author of *The Initiation of Christ*, had acquired an extraordinary reputation for holiness after being murdered by T. S. Eliot in Canterbury Cathedral.[6] Chaucer's Canterbury pilgrims, better known as the Prodigal Fathers, tell Canterbury tales (in iambic vexameter couplets, with the usual tale-rime stanza) as they canter to Canterbury on their annual pilgrim's progress to St. Thomas's Canterbury shrine. Best loved is "The Night's Tale," a bedtime story featuring Chaucer's favorite cocktails, Chauntecleer and Pertelote.[7]

About this time Pearl the Poet, presumably female and therefore probably a nun, wrote *Sir Gawain and the Green Girdle*, a palincest[8] relating how Sir Gawain, the Green Knight, was first beknighted and afterwards, clad in coat of male, departed on his *horse de combat* in quest of the Holy Grail. Other pious poets of the period include the Peerless Plowman, author of *The Vision of Sir Launfal*, a knight-

---

6. See *The Dictionary of Christian Iniquity*.
7. In Chaucer all moral judgments must be held in obeyance; but it is difficult to ignore his inability to spell. He was but poorly acquainted with Modern English, and his shaky grasp of English orthography has caused much confusion from his day to ours.
8. An incunabulum with erasures.

arrant who joined the Crusades[9] and died of salvation en route to the Holy Land; and John Gore, the Black Death, who met a gruesome end when he was excommunicated by the papal bull.[10]

During the Muddle Ages the monks and nuns lived in a state of unbridled celibacy. At Cambridge Mass John the Gaunt and Charles the Bald, shunning all venal sin, communed with St. Thomas More, St. Thomas Browne, St. Thomas Beecham, and sundry others of the clerical choler; while Charlie the Chaplain chanted "Gloria in Excelsior" to Edward the Confessor, and St. Vincent Millay, clad in coat of alms, helped St. Bonyface (Monk Lewis) found the Order of the Grey Friers. Medevil religious zeal was further expressed by John Wycliff, of Dover, who exhausted thousands of sinners to repentance. But when Wycliff translated the Old Testament into the New, he was condemned as hereditary and burned as a steak.[11] Thereupon several "University Wits" in-

9. An attempt to recapture Palestrina from the Turks.
10. A cow kept at the Vacuum to supply milk for the Pope's children.
11. Other medevil martyrs were William Tyndale, an early British physicist, who was condemned for hearsay; and John Huss, leader of the Hussars, who was condemned for consorting with republicans and sinners.

UNBRIDLED CELIBACY

Mahatma Dante, author of *The Divine Comedy*,
finds Beatrice out on a limbo
Courtesy of Lord Inkling

stigated the so-called Pedants' Revolt, prompting Henry VI Part III to voice a classic truth: "The pedants are revolting."

Religious fanaticism found expression also in medevil philosophy and drama. St. Thomas Aquinas' treatment of logic, ethics, and ascetics in *Summa Theologica* is the crowning achievement of Muddle Latin literature. In discussing Apostolic Secession St. Thomas (an idealistic monist) and Dunce Scotus (a realistic duelist) split countless hares with the Jewish rabies over how many angels could dance at once on pins and needles.

Such debates appeared frequently in the mystery plays, miracle plays, and other dumb shows of the period. Chief among medevil dramatists was Mahatma Dante, whose *Divine Comedy* has become the divine tragedy of all time. In three acts ("Hell," "Purgatory," and "Heaven") Dante described his love for Beatrice, the Blessed Damozel, revealing how he secured permission to go to hell, and how upon his arrival he found Beatrice out on a limbo. Living in the fourteenth century, Dante was at once a pre-Raphaelite and a forerunner of the Renaissance. With one foot he stood in the Muddle Ages, while with the other he hailed the dawn of a new day.

CHAPTER THREE

Wolf-Gathering

A domino. . . .

—Gamester's Latin Prayer

HAT LITERARY PERIOD which lapsed from Chaucer to Shakespeare is now known as the Baron Period of English culture, since barons who were not themselves barren married baronesses who were, of course, especially barren. Throughout those Dark Ages England was known as the Dark Continent. English writers, now wolf-gathering, forsook Beowulf, Cynewulf, and the Big Bad Wolf for the less lupine joys of the printing press, the wine press, and John Skeleton, whose ghastly *Skeleton in Armor* is the only incunabulum now in the closet of the East Bronx Public Library.

Most familiar to the student of the Baron Period is the popular ballad. Two types of ballads, both of French origin, dominated the late Muddle English literary scene: the *ballet doux* and the *ballet ruse*.

ANESTHETIC DANCING

The ballet doux and the ballet ruse
By kind permission of Lady Spinifex

Each was a form of anesthetic dancing, and each employed such devices as autonomy, mnenotony, schenectady, illiteration, and eternal rhyme.[1] Such great ballads as "The Fox and the Wolf" and "Little Red Robin Hood," by Wolfhound von Eschenbach, an extremely Low German of the fifteenth century, immediately suggest "Barbarous Allen," "Kemp Malone," "The Twa Corpses," and other cuckoo songs by Old Mother Goose, author of *The Golden Egg*. Even more brilliant is Thomas Rhymer's "Owl and Florence Nightingale," a satire on crows, pigeons, ravens, nightingales, and other eavesdroppers:

> Quoth the owl: "To wit, to who?"
> Corrected Florence: "To wit, to *whom?*"
> Quoth the raven nevermore.

Balladmongers were the only memorable writers of the Baron Period, the rest being religious.

During the fifteenth century certain tribes of monads (Mongrels and Tartans) invaded Russia from the region of the Caucus Mountains and established the fabulous Golden Hoard under the iron rule

---

1. Both derived from twelfth-century *fabliaux*—brief, lewd antidotes usually involving animal behavior of some kind.

of Kubla Khan. In 1453 these Vandals (variously known as Goths, Ostrogoths, Visigoths, Demigoths, and Osteopaths) plotted the Fall of Constantinople and the Rise of the Italian Renaissance. At this time Italy was ruled by Machiavelli, the Black Prince. Skilled in all forms of arts and craft, Machiavelli, a true virtuoso-and-so, promoted the study of Aristotle, Pluto, and Isosceles; and later, acting in the guise of the House of Guise, he built the Painter's Palace of Pleasure, where one might have beheld the splendor of Archipelago's murals (now on the dome of the Sistine Madonna), or the even more striking portraits of Rubens, whose keen interest in the female nude led him to be known as the father of the Renaissance. When one views the canvasses of Andrea del Sarto, a designer of women whose reach unfortunately exceeded his grasp, one instantly recalls Fra Flippo Flippi, whose "Adoration of Virgil" is surpassed only by Fra Michael Angelico's "Jewels of the Madonna."[2] Later in the century Italian influences pervaded England, where two cultural ambassadors, Count Vermicelli and Vis-

---

2. This celebrated picture, though scarcely more than a pigment of the artist's imagination, now hangs in the Palace Athena.

count Macaroni, introduced spaghetti, promoted pizza on the piazza, and otherwise italicized the British populace.

About this time Martin Luther, a priest dressed in the garbage of a monk, was arrested for selling indulgences on the streets of Rome without a license. For his doctoral degree this German scholar had written ninety-five theses (with footnotes), none of which had been published, but all of which had been foolishly tacked on the doors of Wittenberg Cathedral. Provoked by this *ex cathedral* defiance of Cannon Law, Pope Pontifex IX instantly excommunicated Luther from the Holy Roman Empire. But Luther girded his lions and deified the Pope. After a Diet of Bologna and a Diet of Worms, followed by Eau de Cologne, he was naturally [*sic*] for a Reformation, and, filled with riotous indignation, he slew the papal bull and proclaimed his doctrine of transubstantiation by faith. "If any man smite thee on the right cheek," he cried, "smite him on the other also!"[3]

In the light of the Italian Renaissance and the

---

3. See Ferdinand Bull, "Was John Bull the Papal Bull? Was the Papal Bull a Sitting Bull?" in *Igneous Loyola and the Spanish Imposition* (Madrid, 1492).

Protestant Revolt, England found it wise to choose a house of a different color. For three decades she had been ravished by Wars of the Roses. The powerful Robber Barons, astutely observing that "A rose is a rose is a rose," found the white rose of the House of Lancaster and the red rose of the House of York barely distinguishable and fought the Thirty Years' War to settle the difference. At last, convinced at Boswell Field that a house divided against itself cannot stand, and that a rose by any other name would smell as sweet, the barons invited the House of Tutor to the British throne. Accordingly Henry VIII (Prince Hal) was given full reign, and at the suggestion of his prime minister, Oliver Cromwell, he immediately proclaimed himself "Offender of the Faith." Thus by his own efforts Henry increased the population of England by forty thousand. The new King was deeply religious; but he was also disillusioned by the monasteries, where he often preyed; and eventually he divorced Katharine the Great in order to marry Lady Zane Grey, Bluebeard's eighth wife.

Throughout the Muddle Ages England had been Roman Catholic, but with Henry's divorce she became Christian, although the French still obstinately believed in God and remained Catholic. Sacred mat-

THE INVISIBLE SPANISH ARMADA

A view of the English Channel
from Drake's bowling alley
The Spanish fleet approaches at far right
Courtesy of the Misses Sylvia and Myrtle Beach

THE SHORTER CATACLYSM

St. George delivers Lady Zane Grey
from the jaws of the dragon
Courtesy of Miss Agnes Viridian

ters grew more complex with Bloody Mary, who was quite contrary; her zeal for roasting Protestants caused her brief reign to be known as "The Shorter Cataclysm." A distinct tone of unrest pervades *Toddler's Miscellany,* which introduced the euphemisms of John Lyly, the Italian sonnets of Plutarch, and the lyrics of Wyattansurrey.[4]

Meanwhile Christopher Columbus had blazed new trails on the footprints of time. Sailing the ocean blue in search of the United States, he had skirted the Atlantic sideboard, established the State of Virginia,[5] rounded the coast of Florida, discovered Daytona Beach, Palm Beach, and Miami Beach (all inhabited by savages), quaffed at the Fountain of Youth, passed through the Alimentary Canal, touched at the Pancreatic Isles, and thence guided his three frail vessels (the Pinto, the Nina, and the Ave Maria) through the northwest passage to India:

> Breaking the silence of the seas
> Among the farthest Hesperides.

In India he consulted the Taj Mahal, traversed the wiles of the Ganges, and braved such ferocious beasts

4. A lyric is a song to be sung by a liar.
5. Named for the Virgin Mary.

as the rhinostrich, the larynx, the javelin, the criterion, the white elephant, the peccadillo, and the boomerang.[6] Unfortunately fifty of his men were trapped in the infamous Black Hole of Calcutta with one small widow, from which only four emerged alive.

Incensed, Queen Elizabeth demanded that English explorers at once circumnavigate the known universe. Accordingly Sir Walter Scott became undertaker of the Last Colony of Roanoke; Will Rogers founded an insane asylum in Rhode Island; and Peter Minuet, drawn by favorable climactic conditions, discovered New York for twenty-four dollars. Later, when it appeared that Elizabeth was secretly building castles in Spain, Philip II, laboring under a false misapprehension, sought to invade England with his Invisible Spanish Armada; but Sir Francis Drake spied him out while bowling and cried, "A sail! A sail!" Fortunately the Spanish ships floundered and were dispensed by a storm. Philip's defeat by Captain Kydd is now known as *The Spanish Tragedy; or, Twenty Thousand Colleagues Under the Sea.*

6. *Ibex*, p. 23.

CHAPTER FOUR

The She-Wolf

The specious times of great Elizabeth.
—Tennyson

O HER LOYAL SUBJECTS Queen Eliza-beth was universally known as "The Virgin Queene." As a queen she was highly successful. Clever and beautiful, with red hair and freckles, she was also wise and vir-tuous, and therefore she never married, but instead swore like a sailor and painted herself and other things. Often she threw her spinsterhood into the sea of European politics, and, though neither Ro-man nor Catholic, she more than once threatened to excommunicate all those who would not swear that she was the Pope. She was so fond of dresses that she was seldom seen without one on. One day, however, when she rode through Coventry with *nothing* on, Sir Walter Scott offered her his velvet cloak, upon which occasion Edmund Spenser con-ceived his masterpiece, *The Virgin Queene*. Only six of the twelve proposed cantos of this poem have survived; but Dr. Johnson's comment is still final: "Sir," he once declared, breathing through his diagram, "one should dispense with any dispenser of Spenser."

In order to appreciate Elizabethan drama one must first understand fully the Greek drama of the Age of Pericles. Following the victory of Thesis and Thesaurus at the Battle of Salami (one of Ceasar's Pubic Wars), three Greek tragedians (Aeschylus, Socrates, and Euripides), having first consulted the Delphic Oracle (a volcano giving amphibious answers), settled near the Apocalypse in Athens to produce classical tragedy. In strict classical tragedy (for example, the works of Mephistopheles, Metamorphosis, and Methuselah) all action occurs offstage.[1] Following this exacting standard Socrates wrote seven terrible tragedies, all observing the three unities (time, space, and action), and all expressing his well-known philosophy that "No man knows anything." Socrates was a Stoic (a disciple of Zero) who thought of himself as a fly sent to gad about Athens; but he was also a heavy drinker, and in time hemlock corrupted his morals.

1. The plays of Meander were lost.

It was to the Greeks and Romans that Elizabethan dramatists looked for guidance in their early tragedies. The greatest Elizabethan playwright was Christopher Morley, a truly first-rate dramatist but for Shakespeare. In *Doctor Faustus* Morley's tragic flaw was his failure to provide a tragic flaw, and for this tragic flaw he was sharply criticized by Frances Bacon, a sister of Roger Bacon and the only reputable female writer of the period.[2] Frances Bacon founded *The Atlantic Monthly,* in which she introduced the now famous Shakespeare-Bacon Controversy, also known as Bacon's Rebellion. For many years this controversy posed a mute question; but it has finally been established, on the basis of infernal evidence, that Shakespeare never wrote Shakespeare's plays. Actually they were written by another man of the same name.[3]

William Shakespeare was the greatest dramatist the world has yet to produce. He came of a very respectable family and was, through no fault of his own, born poor but honest on a hot and paltry day in 1564, presumably on his birthday, near Suffix, En-

2. She died of whopping cough following an overdose of acrobatic spirits of pneumonia.
3. *Ibidem.*

THE SHAKESPEARE-BACON CONTROVERSY

Shakespeare (*left*) faces Bacon (*right*)
as the Earl of Oxford looks on
Courtesy of the Honourable Mrs. Upshott

gland, while his parents were travailing abroad. In extreme youth, having already marred Anne Hatchaway, the Merry Widow, he settled at Windsor with his eight merry wives, where he remained until 1611, when he removed to Stratford-on-Auburn, more commonly known as the Deserted Village. Shakespeare never made much money, and he is remembered today chiefly for his plays, most of which have, unfortunately, been dramatized. In early manhood he wrote *Love's Labour's Lust*, to be followed shortly by *As You Lack It* (a high comedy), *The Merchant of Venus* (a low comedy, featuring the villainous Skylark), and *Anatomy and Coleoptera* (a comedy of errors):

> Age cannot wither nor costume stale
> Her indefinite virginity.

In later manhood he wrote *Othello* (the first domestic tragedy), *King Lear* (the last domestic tragedy), and *Hamlet* (a tragedy of errors). Shakespeare betrayed women brilliantly: he created female characters with a stroke of his pen, and it is impossible to find a Hamlet among them. Although he was a dramatist of vast proportions, he sometimes also wrote poetry: *The Rape of Lucretius* was inspired by the works of Seneca, a Roman prefix under Emperor Trojan. Shakespeare wrote almost exclusively in blank verse (unrhymed ironic pentameter); and his plays often present a fool—sometimes Shakespeare himself.

Following her death in 1603 Queen Elizabeth graciously relinquished her throne to James I, a Scottish Chaucerian living in Hollywood Castle and reputed to be "the wildest fool in Christendom." James I believed in the Divine Rite of Kings, and after writing the St. James Bible he became known as "Author and Finisher of the Faith."

The St. James Version of the Bible has been called "the noblest monument of English prose." A glance at Bartlett's *Family Quotations* reveals how many Bibulous passages have become part of our daily speech. In the Five Books of Moses, written on the famous Twelve Tables, we learn how Cain raised Cain against Abel; how Jacob, son of Aesop, stole his brother's birthmark; and how Moses led the children of Egypt into the Promised Land of Canada. It was on this memorable journey that Lot's wife was sent into the desert to become a pillar of salt by day and a pillar of fire by night. Shortly thereafter the greatest miracle in the Old Testament occurred when Joshua told his son to stand still and he obeyed him. Later we read how David the

LOVE'S LABOUR'S LUST

Solomon, Gomorrah, and the Queen of Bathsheba
A scene from "The Rape's Progress"
Now in the National Galley

Psalmist married the Queen of Bathsheba and became the father of Solomon and Gomorrah; how Rabbi Ben Ezra vexed the patience of Jove; how Jonah the Whale swallowed Jude the Obscure; and how Elijah abandoned Elisha, his wife, to go on a cruise with a widow.[4]

4. It was at this time that John the Baptist was beheaded for dancing too persistently with the daughter of Herodotus.

CHAPTER FIVE

The Great Wolf

Sunday is icumen in:
Lewdly sing cuckoo!

—Puritan Motto

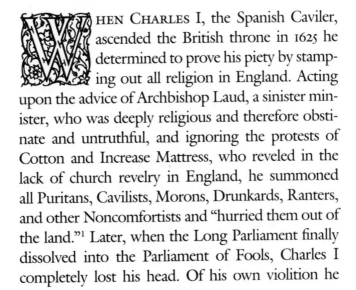HEN CHARLES I, the Spanish Caviler, ascended the British throne in 1625 he determined to prove his piety by stamping out all religion in England. Acting upon the advice of Archbishop Laud, a sinister minister, who was deeply religious and therefore obstinate and untruthful, and ignoring the protests of Cotton and Increase Mattress, who reveled in the lack of church revelry in England, he summoned all Puritans, Cavilists, Morons, Drunkards, Ranters, and other Noncomfortists and "hurried them out of the land."[1] Later, when the Long Parliament finally dissolved into the Parliament of Fools, Charles I completely lost his head. Of his own violition he

1. *Idiom*, p. 67. See Havelock Ellis, *The Psychology of Sects.*

39

summoned the celebrated Rumpus Parliament, by which he was declared unconstitutional, sold into government bonds, and speedily exisled.

The departure of the King marked the commencement of a strange interlewd known as The Interrectum, during which Old Ironsides, Lord Protector of the Commonwealth, and neither a Moron nor a Drunkard, revoked the license with which the Cavilists, or Caviler Poets, had been living their amorous lives. Provoked at being revoked, Captain Andrew Marvell continued living with his coy mistress among the nuns at Appleton House; Abraham Cowley, noted for his metaphysical conceit, was hanged by the Arab dramatist Abou Ben Jonson for not keeping his meter running; and the Rev. John Donne, Dean of Women at St. Paul's, and easily the most physical of the metaphysicals, died while preaching at his own funeral.

Among the leaders of the Puritan Interlewd, John Stuart Milton, the Last Puritan, was a true Renaissance humorist, a poet of epic-making importance, and one of the millstones of English literature. He was to the manor born. While still in infancy his parents read to him the complete works of Shakespeare, Wordsworth, and Ezra Pound. Widely suspected as a veritable progeny of learning, he took all

METAPHYSICAL CONCEIT
Andrew Marvell defies the nuns at Appleton House
A portrait of the author as a young man
From the collection of Christopher Street, Esquire

knowledge to be his providence, chose poetry as his vacation, secured a poetic license, and embarked upon the threshold of a literary career. After a time in Rome, where he paced the banks of the Tiger, gazed at Galileo through his "optick glass," and feasted his eyes on the Holy Sea, drinking it all in, he returned to London, where, fortunately for prosperity, his poetical career was interrupted by twenty years of Civil War.

Milton excelled in all three forms of poetry: lyric, dramatic, and epidemic. He was a poet in all five senses, though he was sometimes deficient in taste. In "Lycidas" he mourned the death of his friend King Edward through the allegorical disguise of St. Peter and Ole Man River. In his "Sonnet on His Third Birthday," which is indeed neither sonnet nor sequence, he followed the form of the Italian, or Pedestrian, sonnet rhyming *abbaabbadecade*. But the triumph of his early years came with "Il Spenseroso," a piece of Spenserian criticism in Italian anapestilent tetrimeter.

Milton's prose tends to be dull and monogamous, not to say mute and inglorious, and his verse is almost totally blank. But in *Areopagitica*, modeled on Cicero's ovations to Catiline, his conception of liberty becomes most striking: "I cannot praise a

fugitive and cloistered virgin, unexorcised and un-
breathed, that never sallies out and sees her adver-
sary, but slinks out of the race." In the light of these
lines Milton's marriage to Mary Powell assumes the
greatest impotence. The unadulterated truth of the
marriage will perhaps never be known; but it is certain that after the wedding bands were issued, the
marriage was solomonized, Milton kissed his bride
(a touching scene), and the happy pair settled in
holy bedlock. Mistress Mary constituted the last lap
of Milton's maiden voyage on the highway of matri-
mony. He found her unbearable, inconceivable, im-
pregnable, even inscrutable, so that, though he considered marriage a holy ordnance, he finally agreed
with Caesar: "Beware the brides of March."[2]

In his blindness Milton depended on his daughters (Comma, Camilla, and Cedilla) for assistance in
producing his most imperishable creation, *Paradox
Lost,* which, although not a sonnet, is an admirable
piece of verse and one of the best-punctuated poems
in English. Unlike the epics of Homer, Virgil, and
other epicures, *Paradox Lost* takes its inspiration
from Holy Wit: Milton frequently uses the Bible
as a frame of reverence. The poetical illusions are

2. Polly Andry, *Milton's Conception of Marriage.*

NEO-CHASTICISM

Nell Gwyn bathes in the Serpentine
By kind permission of Lady Pence-Farthing

scared when not profane; and the style is grand. For a scholarly appraisal of Eve's temptation, stumble, and fall one should consult Keats's "Eve and St. Agnes," which pictures Ariel, an acute angel, and Uriel, an obtuse angel, at the precise moment when Eve, gazing on Satan with wild-eyed amusement, plucks Adam's apple.

Before the publication of *Paradox Lost* the Puritan Interlewd had ended with the Grate Fire of London and the Restoration of Charles II, the Rich Young Ruler, whose coronation was greeted with shouts of applause in Pepys's dairy and throughout London.[3] With the Carolingian Period officially commenced the Age of Innocence Abroad, during which the English court became decidedly French and therefore wicked. France was then in her Golden Age under Louis D'Or, the Prodigal Sun, and his wife, Edith of Nantes; and Bonnie Prince Charlie, pleased with this state of extreme culture, introduced into England such French innovations as high heels, powdered whigs, plaster of Paris, courtesans (*les syphilides*), Neo-Chasticism, and the Bucolic Plague.[4] It

3. "And so to bedlam."
4. Aimée de la Vache, "The Plague's the Thing," *RFD*, 1665 (1665), 16–65.

was indeed a scandalous time; but when one considers the age as a hole, everything falls into place.[5]

To Charles's loose morals Nell Gwyn, a clown in Piccadilly Circus, was, broadly speaking, only the natural accompaniment. This ravishing creature pulled the wolf over the king's eyes. She was, figuratively speaking, the positive symposium of pulchritude; and in addition she featured one of the most beautiful rhyme schemes in English literature. Even her participles dangled. It would, of course, have been virtuously impossible for Charles to marry this loose liver, for Little Nell was, roughly speaking, a woman of the wrong world. In his hand the thing became a strumpet.

Shortly thereafter England decomposed Charles II and invited William the Silent (William Tell) to the British throne. William gladly accepted England's invitation (the Overture to the Flying Dutchman), and nervously ascended the throne by the Act of Circumcision. Once in London, William promptly passed the so-called Glorious Resolution, according to which: (1) no man might be beheaded without his own consent; and (2) no king could order taxis without permission from Parliament. William

5. John Crowe Ransom, *The World's Bawdy*.

THE BUCOLIC PLAGUE
A view of the Houses of Parliament from Golders Green
Pepys's dairy in the foreground
Courtesy of Mademoiselle Aimée de la Vache

subsequently passed the so-called Act of Onion, according to which: (1) England, Scotland, and Iceland would join to form the Untied Kingdom; and (2) Britain would henceforth be a limited mockery, in which only one man could be king at a time.

In seventeenth-century England the hand of man set foot for the first time in the forest of "The New Science."[6] Through his microscope the Italian stargazer Galileo had already split infinity, discovered the Murky Way, and proved that the earth makes one resolution every twenty-four hours. Inspired by his celebrated dictum, "I am; therefore I think" (which actually puts Descartes before the horse), the French *philosophe* Descartes, collaborating with his wife, Algebra, invented plain and stolid geometry. In England Sir William Harvey invented the circulation of the blood; and Sir Isaac Walton, having cultivated the growth of his own apples, invented gravity. At Walton's insistence Parliament officially enacted the Law of Gravity in 1687; and it is still in operation, though noticeable chiefly in the autumn when apples are falling from the trees.[7]

6. See *The Dictionary of Natural Biography*.
7. For further details leaf through *The Encyclopedia Botanica*.

CHAPTER SIX

Wolf Worthies

Hic sex rex.

—Virgil

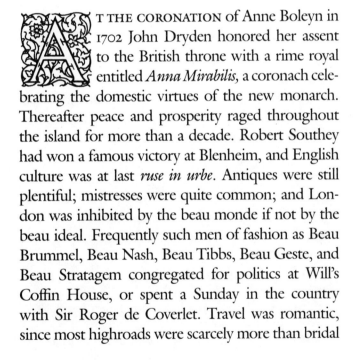 T THE CORONATION of Anne Boleyn in
1702 John Dryden honored her assent
to the British throne with a rime royal
entitled *Anna Mirabilis,* a coronach cele-
brating the domestic virtues of the new monarch.
Thereafter peace and prosperity raged throughout
the island for more than a decade. Robert Southey
had won a famous victory at Blenheim, and English
culture was at last *ruse in urbe.* Antiques were still
plentiful; mistresses were quite common; and London was inhibited by the beau monde if not by the
beau ideal. Frequently such men of fashion as Beau
Brummel, Beau Nash, Beau Tibbs, Beau Geste, and
Beau Stratagem congregated for politics at Will's
Coffin House, or spent a Sunday in the country
with Sir Roger de Coverlet. Travel was romantic,
since most highroads were scarcely more than bridal

paths. And Richard Brinsley Sheraton, playwright and politician, had with characteristic *esprit décors* elevated interior design to a fine art. It was indeed England's Golden Age *par excellence.*

To commemorate the accession of George I and the House of Hangover in 1714, Alexander Pope translated Virgil's *Georgics* and wrote an epistle to Dr. Arbuthnot. Formerly the Popes had resided in Augustan Rome, and since Alexander was the first Pope to reside in England, the Age of Pope is usually called the Augustan Age, in recognition of Pope's indebtedness to St. Augustan. For centuries Latin literature had been a source of unspeakable satisfaction to millions, and Pope, believing that Virgil is its own reward, established the Neo-Classical School in London to perpetrate Rome's legacy to the Western world. Although the school was frequently closed for altercations, it did much to immortalize such Romanesque classics[1] as Polonius, Octopus, Calculus, Leviticus, Parnassus, Aesophagus, Fetus, Euphonius, Livid, and Marius the Epicurean.[2]

1. "Works to be studied in class" (*ODE*).
2. Classical art, Pope said, is the art of Handel, Bach, Beethoven, and Brahms. It is indeed thrilling to hear Beethoven's "Erotica" Symphony or the *andante inferno* from his Suite for Oboe, Baboon, and Strings; but Beethoven

RUSE IN URBE

A Sunday in the country with Sir Roger de Coverlet
Courtesy of Optimus Swivett, Esquire

In 1712 Jacob Tonson published Locke's "Rape of the Pope," a bit of light society verse relating the melancholy story of a flirt whose coiffure was ruthlessly disheveled during a card game at Hampton Court:

> To flirt is human, to forgive, divine.

Pope firmly believed that the proper study of mankind is man and not woman; he therefore construed Locke's *tour de farce* as a personal affront (the Popish Plot) and retaliated in his didactyllic poem "The Art of Stinking in Poetry," another bit of light society verse, dedicated to Golley Cibber, published at the suggestion of Sir Richard Blackamoor, and now preserved at Scrotum Hall, Yorkshire:

> A little yearning is a dang'rous thing:
> Drink deep, or taste not the Venerean spring.

Later Pope translated Homer's *Idiot* and *Oddity* into impeccable heroic cutlets.[3] Some critics consider

---

is, of course, neither Handelian, Bachanalian, nor Brahmin; and one has only to hear Bach's suggestive "Air for the G String" to appreciate that no romantic classic can be classed with a classic classic.

3. A heroic cutlet is a two-line cutlet with blank verse in each line; it is usually a rather long narrative cutlet relating the

Pope pedestrian because he wrote only in iambic feet; but of all English poets he probably did the most to shape the course of English friction.[4]

Meanwhile Jonathan Swift had won his reputation as a noble savage in *A Tale of a Tub*, where his noble, savage prose literally reeked with satiric truth. Through the daughters of Sir William Temple (Shirley and Villette) Swift had met Stella and Vanessa; but despite *The Journey to Stella* and *Venus and Vanessa* it is still not clear whether Swift, Stella, and Vanessa were married, in love, or verse vice.[5] In *Treasure Ireland*, Swift's answer to the Irish Question, he demonstrated that burlesque has a *broad* meaning, usually involving a take-off of some kind. His triumph, of course, came with *Gulliver's Travels*, a charming collection of nursery tales, in which the Big Indians, Little Indians, and Mohair Indians are eclipsed only by the Yahoos, Wahoos, Voodoos, Tattoos, and Kangaroos.

In similar spirit Daniel D. Foe produced *Robinson*

---

deeds of some great national figure, such as Oedipus' final return to Peloponnesus, his wife, or Achilles' entrance into Troy disguised as a wooden horse.

4. After his death Pope was left with no piece of mind, and he destroyed his letters as discriminating evidence.

5. See George Meredith, *The Amazing Marriage*.

SOFT PRIMITIVISM

A study in backgrounds
The undraped figure is presumably a Wigglesworth
By kind permission of Signorina Angelina Torso

Caruso, the diary of a tenor from Ravenna isolated on a desert island; William Hogarth depicted the human comedy in "The Rape's Progress," also known as "The Prints Charming"; and John Gay in his musical comedy *The Burglar's Opera* burlesqued Macbeth, a notorious highwayman whose wife dies of sleeping sickness in Act V.

Through Henry Fielding's efforts the Licensing Act of 1737 provided that all broadsides be censured by the government. It was Samuel Richardson's *Pamela; or, Virgin Rewarded*, an expostulary novel, that first brought this law into action. Richardson later published *Sir Charles's Grandson; or, Female Difficulties* and *Clarissa Harlot; or, The Mistakes of a Night*. Eventually Laurence Sterne, the Little Minister, purified the tone of fiction in *Tristram Shanty*, a picturesque novel. Fielding himself had paved the way in *Tom Jones; or, The History of a Fondling*, the confessions of an unwonted child, and in *Amelia; or, The Starvation Army*, a biography of General William Booth.

Neo-Chasticism witnessed also the rise of periodical literature. Some of the most conspicuous literary creations of Augustan England first appeared on the pages of *The Harlem Miscellany* and *The*

Ladies' Monthly. In 1709 Addison Steele commenced the *Tatler* and *Spectator* papers, semiweekly periodicals reporting births, deaths, marriages, and other public calamities. Aiming to "bring philology out of the clouds into clubs and coffin houses," Steele published hundreds of familiar essays from which *The New Yorker* can trace direct dissent.

At last Steele died of Addison's disease, but his work was continued by Lady Mary Worthless Montagu, "Queen of the Blues," a millionheiress whose celebrated Persian letters describe her travels in blue stockings in the Near East. Mrs. Montagu was the first woman to be intoxicated for smallpox; she also introduced Dakota figs into the supermarkets of London. In Alexandria she met Rosetta Stone, an early archaeologist, who gave her a key to the ancient Egyptian hydraulics on the Sphinx and Pyrenees.

It was through Mrs. Montagu's introduction that Sir Horrors Walpole, longest letter-writer in England, began his distinguished correspondence with Lady Charlotte Russe of Moscow. Walpole was descended from a long line of ancestors. With Bette Noire, his French wife, he resided at Nightmare Abbey, an ancient gothic ruin on Lake Superior. For some years he studied at Sheraton's School for Scan-

LADY CHARLOTTE RUSSE OF MOSCOW

From the original portrait by Sir Horrors Walpole
Now in the possession of Vodka Countess Kopek

dal, whence he wrote his well-known *Letter from So Ho, a Citizen of the World, to His Friend Ching-Ching the Chinaman.*

English interest in orientalism had commenced earlier in the century with the publication of Adam Smith's *Wealth of Natives.* Thereafter London was invaded by such famous orientals as Formosa and Mimosa, Fling Woo and Water Loo, Chop Styx, Ding Dong, Beri Beri, Egg Foo Yung (a Chinese mandolin), Ho Ho Ho, Yum Yum Yum, Tsk Tsk Tsk, and scores of others too humorous to mention. Through the good offices of Mikado, London emissary of the Japanese Shotgun, Pajama introduced to London drawing rooms his wife Kimono, whom James Boswell found to be an extraordinary example of "soft" primitivism. Dr. Johnson was particularly struck by Rasselas, Prince of Abyssinia, and by Lo, the poor Indian with untutored mind. Later a sharp contrast between oriental and accidental culture became apparent when Sing Sing, formerly known as Sing Sang Sung, introduced to Englishmen the philosophy of Buddha the Pest, and when Hegira, wife of Mohammed, published the *Kodak* at the suggestion of Himalaya, viceroy of the Hindu Marjoram.

CHAPTER SEVEN

The Wolf in Street Clothing

Le style c'est moi.

—Buffoon

OR HALF A CENTURY Dr. Sam: Johnson, Prince of Whales, figured very largely in the London literary world. Even as a child he went to Juvenal Court to answer charges brought against his satires, and later he wrote Lord Chesterfield's dictionary and Boswell's life. To Johnson, a harmless drudge, it was a joy to breathe the Londonderry air. Frequently he wandered bearheaded through each chartered street, or rushed pell-mell down Pall Mall, or took a handsome cab or similar public convenience to his designation in Solo Square. He was indeed a Great Briton. His religion bordered on dietism, though his eating and drinking habits were said to be abdominal. When he was not lunching *al fiasco* with the Duchess of Brixton in Quality Street, he was sharing a bottle of champagne with the Marchioness of Frothmore in Back Street, or chatting with the Countess of Ayrwyck over tea and strumpets in Curzon Street, or gorging Cheshire cheese and chicken coquette with his daughter Irene in Fleet Street.[1] At the Bore's Head Tavern, where he was often put up with for the night, Johnson made many fast friends, among the fastest being Dr. Burney, father of Fanny Brice; Edward Gibbon, whose decline and fall Fanny Brice said was neither Empire nor Chippendale; David Hume ("Praise God! From Hume all blessings flow"); James Boswell, author of *An Account of Corsetry* (with special reference to Anne Bracegirdle); and Oliver Goldsmith, who died of pecuniary embarrassment following publication of "The Deserted Village":

I see the rural virgins leave the land.

On one occasion Johnson rebuked his friend Edmund Burke in polysyllabic terms: "Sir," he said, "you are so bombastic and I am so illiterate that you must elucidate before I can comprehend." Equally polysyllabic was Johnson's famous apology to the Earl of Chesterfield, who combined the morals of a dancing-master with the manners of a whore: "Sir," he said, "the remoteness of Lord Chesterfield's habi-

---

1. Such diversions are now called *Johnsonease*.

tation precludes social intercourse without the aid of equine transportation." Even more polysyllabic was Johnson's account, phrased in long-rolling periods (and commas), of a fire in Golden Square: "Sir," he said, "I rose from my couch to view the conflagration; but before I could arrive on the scene of action, lo, it had been extinguished."

Johnson was a man of peculiar pride and prejudice, and he believed that the population of Scotland was a bit too thick; but he nevertheless toured Scotland and the Silly Islands in 1773 and later published his *Sentimental Journey to the Western Isles of Scotland*. He dined in London in 1784, crowned with honors, and was buried in Westminster Abbey.

Meanwhile English Neo-Chasticism had gone from bad to worst. One Thomas Gray (whose aunt, Lucy Gray, was a cousin of Wordsworth on his maternal side) had visited a romantic churchyard at Stoke Poges, where he had produced Gray's elegy, opening with that immortal line:

The curfew shall not ring tonight.[2]

---

2. Inspired by her classic mews, Gray then wrote "An Ode on the Death of a Favorite Catfish Drowned in a Tub of Goldfinches," a witty ditty inscribed to an unwary kitty, Puss in Boots, who at the time of her drowning was evidently not up to scratch.

DECLINE AND FALL

Neo-Chasticism goes from bad to worst
By kind permission of Miss Arabella Cope

Shortly thereafter a very romantic poet named Edward Young, seeing Gray's effigy in the country churchyard, wrote his thousand and one *Night Thoughts*, among them "Twelfth Night" and "The Night Before Christmas." Later, working from a unanimous source, Thomas Percy, who suffered from Gray's allergy, furthered the romantic cause with Gray's eulogy, which promptly inspired the forgeries of James Macpherson, the Old Pretender, author of *Ossian*. Although no one knew at first whether Ossian was alive and composing or dead and decomposing, Dr. Johnson, openly hostile to all things Sottish, dismissed Macpherson's poems as counterfeit. "Any poet," he declared, "in a storm."

Later Thomas Chatterton, the Young Pretender, published his *Rowdey Poems* (the Purloined Letters) under false pretenses; and following his marriage (for bitter or for worse) to a Miss Fortune, this "Marvelous Boy," fed up with having nothing to eat, drank a love potion (milk of amnesia) and died of suicide. Poverty was also the lot of Robert Burns, son of a coal minor, who revealed his uncommon love for uncommon animals in "To a Louse":

> Hail to thee, blithe spirit!
> Bird thou never wert.

In this penetrating apostrophe to his household pest Burns wraps his louse in philosophy to make it more palatable.[3] Animal animus animates also the work of William Cowper, a nervous wretch, who was adjudged a congenial idiot after the publication of *Only Hymns*. Another very romantic poet, William Blake, shared Cowper's humanitarian impulse in his futile desire

> To see a word in a grain of sand,
> And maternity in a wild flower.

In youth Blake wrote *Songs of Innocence*; after his marriage he wrote *Songs of Experience*.

Already Sir Walter Raleigh's *Lay of the Last Minister*, an attack on clerical immorality, had inspired such novelists as Henry Brooke (the fool of quality), Henry Mackenzie (the man of feeling), and Ann Gothica Radcliffe (the mistress of Udolpho). Mrs. Radcliffe, born in the Castle of Otranto on Lake Eerie, grew up at Northanger Abbey near Heathcliff and attended the Graveyard School in the City of Dreadful Night. Her life was rapt in mystery. After founding Radcliffe College she invented the exclamation point and became the bride of Frankenstein. As undisputed head of that vast mob of the unen-

3. See Burns's autobiography, *Of Mice and Women*.

EXCLAMATION POINT
Ann Gothica Radcliffe,
mistress of Udolpho, bride of Frankenstein,
and founder of Radcliffe College
Courtesy of Lady Jane Austen

joyed, she was surely more to be pitied than censored; but Lady Jane Austen censored Mrs. Radcliffe freely in the genial but vitreous humor of her three novels of manors, *Pride*, *Prejudice*, and *Persuasion*.

With the rise of romanticism came also the rise of revolution. By 1750 England's colonies in America had become a melting pot in which sundry revolting masses were confused to form a new society and a new culture. Aroused by the English pamphleteer Thomas Paine, a rare individual obsessed by common sense, Americans demanded freedom from speech, freedom from religion, and *e pluribus union* for all men, regardless of race, creed, color, or sex. When Lord Brute, a benevolent despot, passed the so-called Stampede Act in 1765, Paul Revere took his famous ride with Henry Wordsworth Longfellow; and George Washington, aided by "Lighthouse" Harry Lee and abetted by Wordsworth's "Revolution and Independence," attended a grand tea party[4] in Boston harbor, where he erected the Statue of Liberty and adopted the Declaration of Independence, according to which: (1) everyone should be forced to do exactly as he, she, or it pleased; (2) everyone was as good as everyone else, and in most

4. EATS: 1773.

cases a great deal better; and (3) America would henceforth be "one nation, invincible, with liberty and justice for all":

> Where Freedom slowly broadens down
> From President to President.[5]

Fortunately the British Prime Minister, Sir William Pitt, being bilingual, spoke both English and American. Cessation of hospitalities came with Cromwell's surrender at Yorktown, where Washington uttered his oft-quoted remark: "Our rebels now are ended."

Meanwhile on the European continent Austria, Russia, and Prussia were still at opposite Poles. Forming the famous Triple Alliance, they perpetrated the Petition of Poland, convinced (with Marie Antoinette) that "The Polish have no polish." When Jean Jacques Rousseau confessed his belief in letting nature take its course, Charlotte Brontë murdered Murat in his bath in the *robe de chambre* of the Palace de la Concorde; Sydney Carton was ultraviolated for treason; and "La Marseilles" (the battle hymn of the republic) became the theme song of the French Revolution. All over Europe crowned heads trembled in their shoes. In Paris untold thousands were

5. No reflection is here intended on the present recumbent.

guillotined, and since these deaths usually proved fatal, the Rain of Terror is generally regarded as the Age of Reason. Later Lord Nelson defeated Napoleon in a great navel engagement at Trafalgar Square. "Is this the face that launched a thousand ships?" inquired Napoleon when (at the Peace of Amends) he was exiled to St. Elmo. Napoleon's exile was his "Achilles' hell." Having published his Code Napoleon (the code of many colors), he executed a threatening letter signed in blood (the scarlet letter), passed through the British blockhead into Spain, crossed the Pyramids into France, joined the French Legend of Honor in Paris, and finally met his Waterloo.

CHAPTER EIGHT

The Warp and the Wolf

A wolf's a wolf for a' that.

—Burns

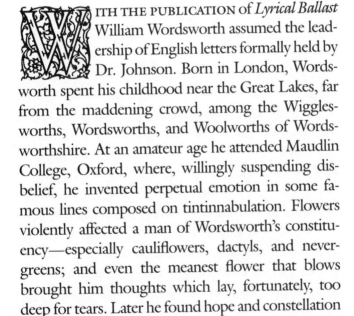ITH THE PUBLICATION of *Lyrical Ballast* William Wordsworth assumed the leadership of English letters formally held by Dr. Johnson. Born in London, Wordsworth spent his childhood near the Great Lakes, far from the maddening crowd, among the Wigglesworths, Wordsworths, and Woolworths of Wordsworthshire. At an amateur age he attended Maudlin College, Oxford, where, willingly suspending disbelief, he invented perpetual emotion in some famous lines composed on tintinnabulation. Flowers violently affected a man of Wordsworth's constituency—especially cauliflowers, dactyls, and nevergreens; and even the meanest flower that blows brought him thoughts which lay, fortunately, too deep for tears. Later he found hope and constellation in nature. Following his marriage to his sister Doro-

thy (the Lady of the Lake) he assumed the name of "Daddy Wordsworth" and speedily became one of England's most prolific writers. Wordsworth gave his reader his word's worth: he frequently wrote poems and prefaces, and sometimes he wrote literature. In his "Ode on Imitations of Immorality from Regulations of Early Childhood" he maintained that rural life is found chiefly in the country. His most famous mistake (a truly pathetic fallacy) appeared in "The Solitary Raper," composed by the seaside near Cathay: "The child," he wrote, "is the father of the man."

It was Wordsworth's coevil, Samuel Taylor Coolidge, who explored the genus of Elizabethan drama in his *Caricatures of Shakespeare's Plays* and related the misfortunes of Silas the Mariner in "The Ancient Marine." John Livingston Loews in *The Road to Timbuktu* suggested that the key to this poem lies in Widener Library. He found the secret of Coolidge's exquisite music in his admiral handling of synonyms,[1] in his unrivaled exploitation of mixed metaphors and implied smiles, in his supernal machinery, in his vivid tropical allusions, and in his sensitive appreciation of the Goethe *Dämmerung*.

1. "Words having two meanings and spelt two ways" (*ODE*).

The Warp and the Wolf

Williams Jennings Byron, author of "Thanatopsis," is considered "the playboy of the Western world." As a child he was called Harold, but at school he became known simply as the Wolf. At Harrow he played Rugby, served on the tennis team, and gambled on the village green with Bella Donna, his fiancée, an Italian lady of English distraction. If Lord Byron had one fault, it was a slight tendency to adultery. Convinced that "A miss is as good as her smile," he took women as a matter of coarse and was frequently up to his neck in cupidity.[2] When he finally married his first cousin (the Lady of Chillon), the belles of London peeled forth. But once united in the holy bonds of acrimony, the Byrons moved from Bond Street to Tobacco Road, where, after that first fine careless rupture, they conducted their affairs amid all the unadulterated lust practicable in a private household. On the morning after the appearance (by fair means or fowl) of *English Birds and Scotch Retrievers* Byron awoke to find himself, but was disappointed. Later he was exiled to Don Juan, a town in the West Indies, whence he finally escaped to Greece. There, amid the throws of a wild and wolfy love affair, he died in the Battle of Marathon, mourned by count-

2. "State or quality of being Cupid" (*ODE*).

PERPETUAL EMOTION

Lord Byron courts the muse
By kind permission of Lady Inasmuch

less fiends and acquaintances. Psychiatrists now believe that Byron suffered from lycanthropy, as a result of which one is cracked (symmetrically) and imagines himself to be and acts like a wolf. Certainly Byron's sounding brass and tinkling symbols reveal a man less sinned against than sinning; but he was probably a good man underneath. His poetry, penned with ravishing proficiency, embraces all mankind—especially persons of the opposite sex.[3]

Most fragile of all romantic poets was Percy Bysshe Shelley, a victim of abnormal psychology, whom Benedict Arnold once called "an ineffective Anglican flapping his lunatic wings in the void."[4] Shelley was born with an ivory tower in his mouth, requiring immediate surgical removal; for many years thereafter he suffered from mucus of the membrane. His poetry may be described as "strictly platonic," but his private life found best expression in *Promiscuous Unbound*, a tragedy portraying Francesca da Gemini and her incestors. Together with his wife, Mary Wollstonecraft, a lady of equality, Shelley favored the emasculation of women. His belief in Pantherism first appeared in his elegiac poem "Adenoids," a

3. *Id.*
4. Benedict Arnold subsequently died of unethical behavior.

lament for Keats based on Byron's "Lament for Adonais." Unfortunately Shelley died while drowning in the Bay of Spumoni. A simple epithet marks his tomb: "Here lies one whose fame was writ in water."

In his "Ode on a Greasy Urn" John Keats proved himself the most romantic poet in the language. At twenty-five he married a musician named Agnes Dei, a ravaging beauty, and on top of that met a speedy death from tuberoses. The lovely Agnes inspired "Eve and St. Agnes," a narrative poem dedicated to Calliope, Errata, and Uranium. Later the poet's love for La Belle Dame Sans Merci[5] convinced him of the immorality of beauty:

> Beauty is youth, youth beauty,—that is all
> Ye know on earth, and all ye need to know.

But Keats's greatest contribution to English literature is his "Ode to Madame Nightingale," addressed to the famous French opera singer who, filled with the milk of human kindness, nursed to health the British soldiers of the Crimean War.

It was at this time that William Hazlitt made his first acquaintance with poets, Thomas De Quinsey

5. The Belle of St. Mary's.

ABNORMAL PSYCHOLOGY

Shelley flaps his lunatic wings in the void
Courtesy of Miss Roberta Tensing

confessed that he was an English opium-eater, and Charles Lamb, in collaboration with his sister Mary, wrote most of Shakespeare's fairy tales. For his doctoral degree Charles Lamb, the autocrat of the breakfast table, had published *A Dissertation on Roast Pig*, dedicated to the memory of Frances Bacon and written in response to Thomas Hogg, author of *A Dissertation on Roast Lamb*, with special reference to *The Apparition of Mrs. Veal*.

CHAPTER NINE

Dyed in the Wolf

He who laughs least lasts best.

—Shakespeare

N 1837 GEORGE III died of a cerebral hemorrhoid, and Queen Victoria, though asleep at the time, rose to the occasion and promptly ascended the British throne. Thereafter for more than fifty years England flourished in splendid oscillation. With the coming of the Industrial Revolution people stopped reproducing by hand and started reproducing by machinery. Under Lord George the Corn Laws were declared dull and void; a new Poor Law put an end to the long-suffering poor; agricultural progress introduced rogation of crops and irritation of the land; rapid scientific strides substantially relieved woman suffrage, especially in childbirth; and England, now dyed in the wolf, began to manufacture iron and steal. During the Bore War Cecil Rhodes discovered scholarships in the Transvaal, and Rudyard Kipling

UTILITARIAN

Jane Welsh, a wife of the opposite sex,
transmutes souls at the University of Teufelsdröckh
Courtesy of Louise Fallopian, Ph.D.

crystallized British imperialism in his classic *Wee Winnie Winkle; or, The Last Days of Bombay*. Finally, at Queen Victoria's Diamond Jamboree in 1897, an invested choir of two thousand vices rendered "Pomp and Circumstance" before Lord Tweedsuit under the vast unsupported roof of the Crystal Palace. Victoria was the longest queen in British history; at her funeral in 1901 it took eight men to carry the beer.

An early Victorious prose writer of no small extinction was Thomas Carlyle, a Scotsman whose wife, Jane, was Welsh. As professor of Things in General at the University of Teufelsdröckh Carlyle was quarrelsome and dyspeptic, while his wife was of the opposite sex. He was also an intimate friend of Ralph Walden Thoreau, pastor of the First Utilitarian Church in Boston. Famous for his self-reliance, Thoreau preached the transmutation of souls, according to which God speaks to Utilitarians through transoms. It was this doctrine that prompted John Henry Newman to publish his spiritual autobiography, *Masses from an Old Manse*, which explained how Newman, a friend of Cardinal Grosbeak, Cardinal Virtue, and Pope Interdict XII, sold his manse, became a cardinal, and wrote "Lead, Kindly Light." About this time Charles Darwin, Aldous Huxley's bulldog, announced his theory of evolution, according to which "ontology recapitulates philology." Darwin insisted that science is material and religion is immaterial. When Cardinal Newman denounced Darwin from every pulpit in England, Huxley rose to Darwin's defense in *Point Counterpoint*, a textbook on musical theory; and Walter Horatio Pater, one of the sons of Belial and father of the Aesthetic Movement, pronounced Newman "a child in the house." Newman declined to answer ether.

Victorious England also boasted a Dickens, a Thackeray, an Eliot, and a Trollope. In the hands of these eminent Victorians English fiction grew not only by leaps but also by bounds; and with the appearance of Dickens's *Nicholas Nickleby*, the first cut-rate dime novel, English fiction at last came of age. In *Vanity Fair* William Masterpiece Thackeray, editor of *Blockhead's Magazine*, reintroduced into fiction the English humors of the eighteenth century. In *Ramona*, a tale of Savonaromola, George Eliot, brother of T. S. Eliot, foreshadowed *Scenes from Clerical Life*, an exposé of London office conditions; in *The Mill on the Floss*, dedicated to Thomas Love Prufrock, Eliot painted a nostalgic picture of life in

CLASSICAL INIQUITY

From a unanimous source

IN MEMORANDUM

Flush, wife of Robert Browning,
poses against a background of Ravioli and Blanc Mange
By kind permission of the Honourable Mrs. Babbage

an old grisly mill. And in *Quo Vadis?* Anthony Trollope described the persecution of the early Christians by Vesuvius.

Meanwhile Walter Savage Landor, "the grandest old Romeo of them all," had stimulated an interest in classical iniquity which found notable expression in the verse of Tennyson and Browning. Throughout the work of these two poets one finds numerous allusions to Orpheus and Euripides, Amoeba and the Myriads, Cyclone and the Doldrums, and Juno and the Peacock.

Unlike most poets, Alfred Lloyd Tennyson neither smoked, drank, nor took poison. He was scarcely of average age when he published "Crossing the Bar," a poem on the legal aspects of death written in the form of a tribute to the Anti-Saloon League. Later, seeking some momentum of his deceased friend Author Hallam, Tennyson, who was prostate with grief, wrote *In Memorandum* to perpetuate the death of Hallam while drowning across Loch Lomond in 1850:

> 'Tis better to have loved and lost
> Than never to have lived at all.

Robert Browning was so moved by this poem's expiring religious message that he produced a series of dramatic monographs for his wife, Flush, whose less-than-kind father then lived in Barrett Street near Berkeley Square. On their honeymoon the Brownings visited Rome, Triste, Larghetto, and Naples, after which they settled in Ravioli near Blanc Mange, where Browning composed a toccata at Galuppi's and wrote the libretto for Wagner's *Ring and the Book*.[1]

1. Browning's poems frequently achieve a musical effect through his skillful use of osmosis, parabola, anglomania, metabolism, and oxfordmoron.

CHAPTER TEN

Cry Woolf!

Words, words, words.

—Shakespeare

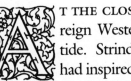T THE CLOSE of Queen Victoria's long reign Western civilization was at high tide. Strindberg's *Peter and the Wolf* had inspired the discords of Stravinsky's *Firecracker Suite;* and Henri Métisse, together with his wife, Claire de Lune, had discovered Modern Art at the Local Color School in Paris. John Greenleaf Whistler had painted his mother; Edward Lear, son of King Lear, had followed Alice through the looking glass; George Bernard Shaw had translated Voltaire's *Candide;* and Arthur Wing Pirandello had shocked Covent Garden with *Sex Characters in Search of an Author.* In London the so-called Wilde Nineties officially commenced with the composition of "The Merry Widow Waltz" and the publication of the works of Shylock Holmes.

Like all great dramatists Oscar Wilde was Irish

85

THE WILDE NINETIES

Audrey Beardsley, Marquess of Middlesex,
frolics with friends from the Irish Free State
By kind permission of Lord Faddeley

and always preferred the Irish Free State. Actually, of course, his ancestry was Bohemian, although he himself eventually settled in Middlesex, where his friendship for Audrey Beardsley became a *fête accompli*. At Oxford Wilde led a life of extreme aestheticism and scandalized the British Empire with his picture of Dorian Gray; when his infamous opera *Salomé and Delilah* was first sung before a British audience, even the Queen shouted "Paris forbid!" and promptly quitted the theater. Wilde later wrote *Lady Guinevere's Fan*, a star-studied farce, and *An Ideal Husband of a Woman of No Importance of Being Earnest*. Accused of vice versa, Wilde was sent to Coventry, a rotten borough, where he soon published *A Ballad Read in Gaol*.

Wilde's plays were posthumorously produced by Sir Max Beerbohm Tree, who encouraged other dramatists of "The English Pail" to follow the footsteps of Ibsen, Shaw, and Coward. Accordingly such Irish playwrights as O'Casey, O'Neill, and O'Henry studied the theories of Sigmund Fraud, analyzed the works of Maxim Gawky, and turned for inspiration to Ibsen and Shaw. Although London has generally preferred Ibsenism and Shavianism to Noel Coward-ice, subourbon New York has always favored Cowardly wit, especially in the pretty prattle of *Hay Fever;*

or, Idiot's Delight and *Private Wives; or, Mr. Brittle Sees It Through.* But some confusion in identity arose with the plays of Thornton Wilder, a popular matinee idyl: Was Wilde Wilder? Was Wilder Wilde?[1]

Meanwhile Modern Poetry had begun in 1857 with the publication of Walt Whitman's *Leaves of Grass*, a volume distinguished for its use of free verse in English. Free verse is (in terms of dollars and sense) free: it costs nothing; it is verse without rhyme or reason, as in Whitman's "Psalm of Myself":

> I contradict myself?
> I contradict myself
> Very well.

This passage requires no comment. Following Whitman's free-verse tradition, Stephen Hart Crane, brother of Ichabod Crane, produced even more radical departures from commonly excepted tradition and jumped off a boat crying: "A poem is like a mute fruit!" Eventually Englishmen were reading the poems of Alfred Noise, Amy Russell Lowell, and Stephen Vincent Millet.

Those who keep abreast of the *Times* know that the field of modern fiction is hopelessly vast and complex. Such critics as Louis Academic and Ber-

1. Wilde *was* Wilder, but Wilder was not Wilde.

SCREAM OF CONSCIOUSNESS
Virginia Woolf confronts the younger degeneration
Courtesy of Dames Mae and Rebecca West

nard de Veto observed freudulent tendencies in the younger degeneration, while others reechoed the defeatism of Spengler's *Decline of Mae West*.[2] In the late nineteenth century William James, Henry James, and Jesse James upset American literature by becoming neutralized British citizens, and it was not until World War I that returning veteranarians fused new blood into contemptuary spirit.[3] After the devastation of the War between the Tates, English criticism entered the so-called Deconstruction Period. Best known among those who remained undeconstructed were Leslie Fiddler, whose "Come Back Ag'in to the Roof, Huck Honey," a griping work, elevated criticism to new heights; William Empson, whose *Seven Types of Pastoral* traced the influence of Beethoven on contemptuary fiction; and Douglas Bush, who was in a league of his own. Any list of significant modern novelists (good, bad, or different) must include Matthew Arnold Bennett; John Erskine Caldwell; Upton Sinclair Lewis, whose *Arrowshirt* introduced Irving Babbitt; and Henry Graham Greene, who at the heart of the matter discovered nothing.

2. Now in William Randolph's hearse.
3. See Henry James's *Aspirin Papers*.

Cry Woolf!

Because Thomas Wolfe has long since gone home again, and because his twin brother, Tom, has proclaimed himself the New Water Poet in his aqueous epic *From the Bath House to Our House*, Virginia Woolf remains the greatest English wolf of the twentieth century. Though she distinctly preferred novels to fiction, Mrs. Woolf made substantial contributions in both fields and through her "scream-of-consciousness" technique did much to bring English fiction to its present flourishing state. Today our forefathers are not living as long as they once did; but unless something very foreseen occurs, it is probable that English literature will continue to flourish until the last syllabus of recorded time.